CHRISTMAS
AT
THE
MOVIES

J.John
Illustrated by Andrew S. Gray

Contents

Prologue

I love Christmas.

The *sight* of decorations, the *smell* of roasted chestnuts, the *sound* of brass bands playing carols – I love it all. If your family is anything like mine, a key ingredient of Christmas is *that* relaxing moment when you settle down on the sofa to enjoy a heart-warming Christmas movie with a smorgasbord of leftover Christmas dinner.

Today there are many different versions of Christmas; different perspectives that point a spotlight on important aspects of the season. The movies featured in this book are some of my festive favourites, but *what if* each movie is simply a side-story to the main script? *What if* the Grinch, Scrooge and Kevin McCallister are no more than extras in the real blockbuster of Christmas?

A Christmas Carol

Our modern Christmas celebration owes an enormous amount to Charles Dickens' popularisation of a food-filled, feel-good, family-focused festival.

A Christmas Carol has been released many times but my favourite is the version with George C. Scott. The plot is focused on Scrooge, a cynical old man who treats Christmas and compassion with the dismissive sneer, 'Bah Humbug!'

He is visited on Christmas Eve by the spirit of former business partner Jacob Marley, then by the spirits of Christmas Past, Christmas Present and Christmas Yet To Come. The spirits reveal to him his self-centred nature and the bleakness of his fate unless he changes his ways.

Convicted by these visions, Scrooge resolves to alter his ways, waking up on Christmas morning changed for good. From now on he is a man overflowing with love, generosity and kindness.

One of the strengths of *A Christmas Carol* is the depiction of Scrooge as a man so consumed by his pursuit of wealth that he has nothing but scorn for friendship, kindness and generosity. He is a miser. It's an interesting word because it was originally linked with 'miserable' and the belief that those who kept their money to themselves were miserable. Scrooge is certainly an unhappy character.

We see Scrooge portrayed as a man who seeks to gain the world but in the process has lost his soul. He is lonely, mean and heartless, but mercy breaks in. Warned by his supernatural visitors, he realises that he has lived entirely for himself, has become miserable and is despised by others. He decides that he needs to change and, with a humble and honest prayer, starts a new life. We see a transformed Scrooge who is a blessing to himself and to others.

A Christmas Carol asks, 'Do we need to change?' At this time of year it's no bad thing to look at our lives and ask, 'What have I become?'

If you do feel that you need to change, what better time than Christmas, which commemorates Jesus Christ being born into the world so we can be born again.

It's a Wonderful Life

It's a Wonderful Life follows the life of George Bailey, born and raised in the typical American small town of Bedford Falls. But he is someone with ambition and imagination who wants to escape, to travel and to achieve something.

Those dreams, however, never materialise. George's commitment to his family and, above all, to his community, means that he spends decades stuck in the town without the obvious visible achievements that his friends and family acquire.

He is a man whose selfless willingness to do little things for others has prevented him from doing big things for himself. One Christmas Eve George's frustration comes to a head with a financial crisis that threatens to send him to prison.

In a fit of angry despair, he goes out to commit suicide. At this point his guardian angel intervenes and, in a nightmarish vision, shows him what his

community and those he loves would have been like if he hadn't existed. In the face of this revelation George realises that his life has indeed been wonderful.

There is much to think about in *It's a Wonderful Life* but perhaps its biggest lesson lies in how we evaluate what we have done.

Society has always celebrated the visible attainments of wealth, power and fame but never more so than today. We are all inclined to measure ourselves by our number of friends (real or virtual), our job title, our bank balance or the size of our house.

God, however, operates on a very different basis and so should we. Looking back this Christmas you may, like George Bailey, reflect on your life and think that actually you haven't done very much. That may very well be you assessing things by the wrong standards.

It's worth remembering that what God values most of all is faithfulness, kindness, generosity and obedience.

Let's be more focused on what we can do for others and less on what we can get for ourselves.

The lesson of *It's a Wonderful Life* is that it's not what you achieve or have that counts, but it's who you are.

The Family Man

A common experience at this time of year is to pick up a Christmas card from an old friend and reflect on the past. Should I have left that job? Should we have stayed at that house? And, if I had, how would things be different?

The idea of having some otherwise hidden aspect of your life supernaturally revealed to you is something that comes up in a number of Christmas films. It also forms the basis of *The Family Man*.

At the start of this film we are introduced to Jack Campbell and his girlfriend Kate in 1987 as he sets off from the States to the UK, leaving her behind.

We then jump forward thirteen years to see that Jack, with Kate long left behind, is now a rich, powerful and successful Wall Street executive who is able to say that he has everything he wants.

Suddenly – and supernaturally – Jack is given a glimpse of the life that could have been his. He wakes up married to Kate, with children and a job as a tyre salesman.

The film shows how Jack adjusts to this life and ultimately realises that being a 'family man' is more rewarding than the wealthier and more powerful life he had on Wall Street.

In the end, Jack is thrown suddenly back to his old life. In an effort to regain the lost happiness he briefly enjoyed, he seeks out his old girlfriend to try to restart their relationship.

It's no bad thing to review our life at Christmas but cautions need to be raised. After all, remembering can often turn into regretting. The 19th-century poet John Greenleaf Whittier wrote:

Of all sad words of tongue or pen,
The saddest are,
'It might have been.'

St Paul, who had a lot to regret, was able to write, 'But one thing I do: forgetting what is behind and straining towards what is ahead, I press on towards the goal to win the prize for which God has called me heavenwards in Christ Jesus' (Phil. 3:13-14).

It's worth learning from our past but we can't live there. Let's press forward with wisdom gained from hindsight to fulfil the potential for the future.

Miracle on 34th Street

My favourite *Miracle on 34th Street* is the 1994 version starring Sir Richard Attenborough.

This feel-good classic tells the heart-warming story of a young girl's desire for a fully functional family, complete with a father and a baby brother. The girl, Susan, confides in Kris Kringle, the kindly old man who is acting as the grotto Santa in the department store managed by her mother.

Kris Kringle, however, believes he is the genuine Santa Claus and his devotion to the cause makes him very popular, leading to record profits for the store. This annoys rival retailers so much that they try to discredit the so-called Santa, leading to a court case in which Kringle and his lawyer try to prove that he is the real thing.

It's a charming film and a delightful window on a long-vanished world of decency and trust.

On the surface, the big question posed by the film is whether Kris Kringle is indeed Santa. Yet there is more to the plot than meets the eye.

At the heart of the film is a discussion of faith: here about Santa Claus but ultimately about something much deeper.

The female lead is a woman whose failed marriage has taught her that in real life fairy-tales go sour. She is cynical and disillusioned and has passed that scepticism on to her 6-year-old daughter who, openly scornful of fantasy and imagination, tries to live entirely by logic and reason.

That disbelieving view is challenged by Kris Kringle and eventually mother and daughter come to believe.

The film sets up two opposing positions. On the one hand we are shown how sceptical, rational thinking can lead to a loss of imagination and hope. On the other we see how faith and imagination can bring the possibility of hope, generosity and love.

Many people believe that Santa manages to get down chimneys to bring presents. Perhaps. What I do know is that if you are prepared to open your heart and mind even the tiniest amount to God, he will enter in and bring the greatest of gifts.

National Lampoon's Christmas Vacation

The plot of *National Lampoon's Christmas Vacation* is that Clark Griswold (played by Chevy Chase) decides that this year his family is going to have 'the most fun-filled old-fashioned family Christmas ever'. He becomes obsessed with organising the perfect celebration, which in his case involves 25,000 Christmas lights, a tree too large for his house and invitations to an utterly dysfunctional extended family.

Inevitably, of course, it all goes terribly wrong and there's all sorts of fun to be had with frosty neighbours, crazy relatives, an invasive squirrel and a cat that spectacularly exceeds its quota of nine lives.

Most of the humour comes from the gulf between Griswold's well-intentioned but naive dream to create the perfect Christmas festivities and the chaotic mess that reality delivers.

Here is the lesson: the danger that the trappings of Christmas – the gifts, meals, decorations and traditions – soon acquire a life of their own and hijack the season. The wrapping paper takes over from the present.

The result is, as Griswold finds out, that you soon find yourself caught up in something you can't control: a monstrous, ever-growing, unstoppable snowball of increasing cost and complexity that crushes everything and everyone in its path. And while we may avoid something of the spectacular calamities in *Christmas Vacation,* we all know of smaller versions.

Perhaps there is a lesson for us in the unpolished and raw setting of the birth of Christ. Perhaps God is saying that at Christmas less really is more.

So this Christmas don't be misled into trying to create the perfect Christmas; it won't work and it isn't necessary.

Create a warm, festive home and be kind and loving to your family and friends. God has put a billion trillion stars up there for Jesus, and that's heart-warming for me.

Home Alone

Home Alone is about how 8-year-old Kevin (brilliantly played by Macaulay Culkin) gets left behind when his rather dysfunctional family leaves for a Christmas vacation in France. And if being left alone was not enough, Kevin has to protect his house from a pair of incompetent burglars.

What most of us remember is Kevin's ingenious defence of his home with the kind of violence more commonly associated with cartoons. Yet there are deeper issues in the film. Take the title *Home Alone:* the friendliest word in the English language attached to one of its most unfriendly adjectives.

The fact is that Kevin's family are not nice either to each other or to him. His first reaction to finding that there is no one else at home is to look straight into the camera and with a triumphant smirk say, 'I made my family disappear!' This Christmas there will be many people who look around at their parents, relatives or even children and

wish they could say the same. Families aren't always fun.

However, it soon turns out that although Kevin spends quite a bit of time enjoying his new freedom and doing all the things that he is not supposed to do, he misses his family.

Partly through interacting with a gruff old neighbour in a church, Kevin reverses his wish for solitude and, with the burglars spectacularly vanquished, his family reappears.

Because our culture has pushed away the 'true reason for the season', we find that 'the family' has often come to replace the Christ Child at the core of the festivities. Although nothing should get in the way of what Christmas is really all about, as Kevin and his parents and siblings come to realise, families are important. This Christmas let's do what we can to bring our family together, and think, too, about those around us who have no family and include them in our celebrations.

How the Grinch Stole Christmas

Sixty years ago Dr Seuss wrote a little children's book, *How the Grinch Stole Christmas!,* as a protest to the commercialism that he thought was destroying Christmas.

It's become astonishingly famous and even those people who have never read the book are aware of the term 'Grinch' for a miserable, sneering person who hates fun and festivity.

The original story is of the Grinch, a solitary, grumpy and spiteful creature who lives outside the town of Whoville. Embittered by the villagers' celebrations, on Christmas Eve he sneaks into the houses and steals all their presents, thinking that this will make them miserable.

The next morning the Grinch, anticipating cries of despair, hears celebration and realises that Christmas is about more than presents.

His miserable heart – 'two sizes too small' – is replaced by a larger one. Returning the presents, he goes into the village and joins the festivities.

The story got the big-budget film treatment in 2000, with Ron Howard directing and Jim Carrey as the Grinch.

Neither the original book nor the film adaptation give any serious consideration to what Christmas is really all about, but they do clearly recognise what it isn't about.

With the Grinch's recognition that Christmas is not something that can be bought, comes a miracle: his shrunken heart grows to three times its original size.

It's hard to argue with the view that, at Christmas, relationships are far more important than things.

The film points to two dangers. The first is that, like the inhabitants of Whoville, you can love Christmas but if you ignore the One who should be central to the season you will end up smothering Christmas with presents, choking it with festivities and strangling it with tinsel.

The second danger is, like the Grinch, to reject the whole thing. But to do that is in the deepest possible sense to throw the baby out with the bathwater. And trust me, at Christmas that's one really important baby.

Christmas with the Kranks

Christmas raises all sorts of issues to do with our lives, our families and our faith. Many of these issues are touched on by films. The issue of community is right at the heart of *Christmas with the Kranks,* a feel-good film based on John Grisham's book *Skipping Christmas.*

The story is of Luther and Nora Krank, played by Tim Allen and Jamie Lee Curtis. Having got their only daughter off their hands, the Kranks decide to skip the Christmas celebrations that they and their neighbours are used to and, instead, go on a Caribbean cruise.

However, their community is appalled at this breach of tradition and the neighbours express their hostility in all sorts of ways.

At the last minute, the Kranks are suddenly forced to change their minds and realise that they desperately need to celebrate Christmas with all the decorations, food and drink. How does the community react? Well it responds with kindness, love and generosity towards them.

That outbreak of grace by the neighbours is reciprocated by an act of forgiveness and kindness by Luther to someone who has been his enemy.

The film, following the book, is pointing out the fact that God is not impressed by how extravagantly we celebrate religious festivals or how dedicated we are to carrying them out. Knowing John Grisham's firm Christian faith, I can't help but wonder whether these words from Amos were in his mind when he wrote the book:

'I hate, I despise your religious festivals; your assemblies are a stench to me. Even though you bring me burnt offerings and grain offerings, I will not accept them . . . I will not listen to the music of your harps. But let justice roll on like a river, righteousness like a never-failing stream!' (Amos 5:21-24).

It's a useful reminder that the validity of any religious faith we might have is not demonstrated in the brightness of our Christmas lights, the height of our tree or the number of Christmas cards we send out, but in how we live out God's grace in our lives.

With Honors

This film's portrayal of 1990s American student life has that really important factor of sticking in your mind once you have watched it.

Set at Harvard University, the story centres on Monty (played by Brendan Fraser), who we meet as a rather arrogant and prejudiced student close to completing his thesis for his degree. His work is of sufficient quality that he should graduate 'with honours'. To graduate from Harvard with honours is the guarantee of a glittering career.

One night disaster strikes Monty's computer and his thesis is lost. As he runs to photocopy his printed version, it falls into the hands of an aggressive homeless man, Simon (Joe Pesci), who offers its return on a page-by-page basis in exchange for food and shelter.

We see how Monty gradually loses his arrogance and prejudice and becomes a nicer person, while Simon is shown to be more than just someone who

can be ignored. Ultimately, in the course of befriending Simon, Monty puts service before honour and pays a very high price.

With Honors highlights the divide in the world: the haves and the have-nots; the big, important people at the top and the little, insignificant people at the bottom; the somebodies and the nobodies.

One important aspect of Christmas in the Bible is that it focuses on little people. Mary and Joseph are two nobodies who turn out to be parents to the biggest Somebody in existence.

This is the outworking of a theme in Mary's great song, the 'Magnificat'. '[God] has scattered those who are proud in their inmost thoughts. He has brought down rulers from their thrones but has lifted up the humble. He has filled the hungry with good things but has sent the rich away empty' (Luke 1:51-53).

With Honors echoes this Christmas theme and sounds a warning: we who find ourselves rich in food, clothes and friends should never forget those who lack the basics. We should care for those who have little and, in the world's eyes, are little – God may have a very different view of them.

The Lion, the Witch and the Wardrobe

C.S. Lewis's classic *The Lion, the Witch and the Wardrobe* is set during World War II. Four children pass through a wardrobe into the world of Narnia, a land frozen in winter for a hundred years by the White Witch. There they encounter the majestic lion Aslan and are involved in the overthrow of the witch and the return of spring.

The story falls into two halves: the first is set in the icebound Narnia under the total control of the White Witch; the second, in which Aslan and the witch confront each other, is set in a thawed spring-like Narnia. These two halves correspond to Christmas and Easter.

Lewis wrote the book in the late 1940s when Britain suffered a continuation of wartime rationing that included fuel. Winters were bitter and miserable; the

coming of spring was something that people eagerly anticipated.

Early in their visit to Narnia the children hear the thrilling rumour that 'Aslan is on the move' and, with it, the hope that his coming will bring spring. Escaping from the White Witch they encounter Father Christmas, a solemn and significant figure who, with Aslan 'on the move' and the weakening of the witch's magic, can enter Narnia once more. After giving gifts he departs with a cry of 'Merry Christmas!' No sooner has he left than the thaw begins.

Lewis's picture of a land frozen in the misery of a seemingly endless winter is a brilliant restatement of the Bible's view of the state of humanity. Created good, we have fallen under the influence of evil. We are spiritually frozen. Yet in that bitter winter God has intervened. Christmas is the powerful declaration that God is 'on the move'. The great thaw, the overthrow of evil, has begun.

The Christmas season brings with it the promise that, although still far away, spring is coming. Christmas is God's promise that, if we trust in the One who was born at this time, spring for our souls is on the way. And this spring will last forever.

Epilogue

I began this booklet by asking two questions:

What if each movie is simply a sidestory to the main script?

What if the Grinch, Scrooge and Kevin McCallister are no more than extras in the real blockbuster of Christmas?

In order to discover the true story of Christmas, it is essential that we go back to the original script – the Bible – to explore the storyboard of what actually happened.

Despite the first people living in a perfect world and walking closely with God, they chose to live their way, rather than God's way. The result was catastrophic: the bond between humanity and God was broken. The trail of brokenness began at that defining moment.

Throughout the Bible, God promised that one day a king would come who would restore the broken bond between people and himself.

Two thousand years ago he arrived. Not as an impressive hero (as many people expected) but as a baby, born into very humble surroundings. The original script tells us that this baby was named Jesus, which means 'God rescues'. Jesus wasn't an ordinary baby, he was God 'in the flesh' – God with us.

By taking our brokenness on himself, Jesus put a roadblock in our trail of destruction and created a way back to God. (You can read more about that at jjohn.com/Christianity). Jesus fixed the broken bond between us and God, and that is why the true story of Christmas is the real blockbuster.

So, how do we respond?

Jesus created a road back to God but, as with any road in life, you can't simply look at it – you have to travel along it. The Christian life is a journey, and the first step is to say 'Yes' to God.

In the world of cinema, a cameo is defined as 'a small but noticeable part in a film or play, performed by a famous actor'.

Today we face a decision: either we allow Jesus to simply be a cameo in our lives, an insignificant character on the periphery, or we choose to make him the main character by saying 'Yes' to God.

If you would like to make Jesus the main character in your life, pray this prayer, adapted from the Christmas carol 'O Little Town of Bethlehem':

O holy Child of Bethlehem,
descend to us, we pray;
cast out our sin and enter in;
be born in us today.
We hear the Christmas angels,
the great glad tidings tell;
O come to us, abide with us,
our Lord Emmanuel!

If you have chosen to make Jesus the main character in your life, can I encourage you to do three things:

1. Tell someone close to you that you have chosen to make Jesus the main character in your life.

2. Start reading the Bible. A good place to start is the Gospel of John.

3. Visit a local church this Christmas to encourage you in your journey of faith.

Happy Christmas!

Published by Philo Trust
Witton House, Lower Road, Chorleywood, Rickmansworth,
WD3 5LB, United Kingdom

www.jjohn.com

British Library Cataloguing in Publication Data

A catalogue record for this book is available from the
British Library

ISBN: 978-1-912326-27-3

Illustrations by Onegraydot Ltd. Andrew S. Gray
www.onegraydot.com

Print management by Verité CM Ltd
www.veritecm.com

Printed in the UK